Holy Spirit
I Pray

*Prayers for morning and nighttime,
for discernment, and moments of crisis*

Jack Levison

author of 40 Days with the Holy Spirit

PARACLETE PRESS
BREWSTER, MASSACHUSETTS

2015 First Printing

Holy Spirit, I Pray: Prayers for morning and nighttime, for discernment, and moments of crisis

Copyright © 2015 by John R. Levison

ISBN 978-1-61261-683-4

Scripture references marked (NRSV) are taken from the New Revised Standard Version Bible, copyright © 1989 by the Division of Education of the National Council of Churches of Christ in the U.S.A., and are used by permission. All rights reserved.

Scripture references marked (THE MESSAGE) are taken from *The Message: Catholic/Ecumenical Edition.* Copyright © 1993, 1994, 1995, 1996, 2000, 2001, 2002, 2013. Used by permission of NavPress Publishing Group.

Scripture references marked (JRL) are the author's own translation.

The Paraclete Press name and logo (dove on cross) is a trademark of Paraclete Press, Inc.

Library of Congress Cataloging-in-Publication Data
Levison, John R.
  Holy Spirit, I pray : prayers for morning and nighttime, for discernment, and moments of crisis / Jack Levison, author of 40 Days with the Holy Spirit.
     pages cm
  Includes index.
  ISBN 978-1-61261-683-4
  1. Catholic Church--Prayers and devotions. I. Title.
  BX2149.2.L48 2015
  242'.8—dc23   2015027829

10 9 8 7 6 5 4 3 2 1

Published by Paraclete Press
Brewster, Massachusetts
www.paracletepress.com
Printed in China

CONTENTS

INTRODUCTION

A book of prayers to the Holy Spirit, even a slender one, is an oddity. While they probably exist, I know of no others. In a modest way, this book may be unprecedented.

Still, the slender book you are holding runs deep along a vein of devotion to the Holy Spirit. The simple prayer, *Veni Sancte Spiritus*, goes all the way back to the Middle Ages: Come, Holy Spirit. It's thought to have been written by Stephen Langton, Archbishop of Canterbury in the 1300s, though we can't be sure. We can be sure that it has had a long life and appreciable impact on the lives of many Christians through the centuries.

You'll find other prayers to the Holy Spirit scattered throughout the landscape of Christianity. There's *O Creator Sancte Spiritu*, which features in ordination services even today, and *O Sancte Spiritus*, as well as a reading of prayers to the Holy Spirit called *Litaniae de Sancto Spiritu* (Litany of the Holy Spirit), in which Christians address the Spirit directly and then repeat, "Have mercy on us." The litany is lovely; here are the opening lines:

Holy Spirit proceeding from the Father and the Son,
    have mercy upon us
Spirit of the Lord, the God of Israel, have mercy on
    us. ...
Adorning the heavens, stable and secure, have mercy
    on us.
Gift and promise of the Father, have mercy on us.
Spirit, through whom we are reborn, have mercy on
    us.
Spirit of sweetness and kindness, sweeter than
    honey, have mercy on us.

Devotion to the Holy Spirit could be deeply personal.
Hildegard of Bingen, a twelfth-century mystic famed
for the beautiful hymns she composed, united mystic
sensibilities with passion in *De Spiritu Sancto*:

Holy Spirit, making life alive,
Moving in all things, root of all creative being,
Cleansing the cosmos of every impurity,
Effacing guilt, anointing wounds.
You are lustrous and praiseworthy life,
You waken and re-awaken everything that is.

These are a few examples of prayers to the Holy
Spirit, but such prayers are rare. As St. Basil, who

lived in Cappadocia—modern Turkey—from 330 until 379 CE, explains in his treatise *On the Holy Spirit*, Christians worship and pray *in* the Spirit rather than *to* the Spirit; they pray, that is, to the Father through and with the Son, in the Holy Spirit. Like Saint Basil, most Christians tend to see the Holy Spirit as a *medium* of prayer and worship rather than an *object* of prayer and worship.

In order to benefit from the unusual prayers in this book, we may need a bit of guidance, which we can find in three words. Not three English words, however, but three *Hebrew* words. The original Jewish Bible, or Christian Old Testament, was written almost entirely in Hebrew, so this is a very good place to start. Don't be intimidated. Each word opens the door to a richer, fuller, more durable use of this book—and experience of the Holy Spirit.

Spirit

The first, of course, is the word translated into English as *Spirit*. The Hebrew word, *ruach* (the *ch* is pro-nounced gutturally, as if you're clearing your throat), had broader shoulders than the English word, *spirit*. *Ruach* could mean a breath, a breeze, a rush of wind, an angel, a demon, the heart and soul of a human being, the waxing and waning of life, a disposition like lust or jealousy, and the divine presence itself.

Just glance at the dramatic vision of the valley of dry bones in Ezekiel 37, which inspired the song "Dem bones gonna rise again," and you'll see what I mean. English translators usually use three distinct words—*breath*, *wind*, and *Spirit*—to translate the single Hebrew word *ruach*. Ezekiel is told, "Prophesy to the *breath* ... 'Come, *breath*, from the four *winds*' ..." (Ezekiel 37:9, NRSV, italics added). The vision ends with the promise, "I will put my *Spirit* within you and you shall live, and I will place you on your own soil" (Ezekiel 37:14, NRSV, italics added). English translations imply that *breath* in-breathed into the bones is somehow different from both the four *winds* that gather and the *Spirit* that will be put into the nation of Israel. But in the original Hebrew, it's all the same word—*ruach*.

Many of the prayers in this book play on the rich resonance of the Hebrew word *ruach*. You may read a prayer with the words *wind* or *Spirit* or *breath*. Remember that these English words are like branches, all of which grow from the thick trunk of an aged tree—*ruach*. Remembering *ruach*, even as you read *breath*, *wind*, and *Spirit*, will render these prayers more resonant, and certainly richer, for you.

Fill

Fill a pitcher with water and you've got an image of filling with the Spirit. The Spirit is poured out on us or into us. When we receive this Spirit, all sorts of things happen to us. We become a new creation (Galatians 6:15; Titus 3:5). We receive the fruits of the Spirit, such as love, joy, and peace (Galatians 5:21–22). We are endowed with gifts of the Spirit—anything from healing to speaking in tongues, from teaching to generosity (1 Corinthians 12:1–11). All of this, and much more, happens through inspiration, when God breathes the Holy Spirit into us, when God *fills* us with the Holy Spirit.

That's not, however, the whole story. The Hebrew verb *fill* (*ml'*) can also mean *filling to the brim from the inside out*. When periods of time are over, for example, they are *filled up*. Jacob's long wait for Rachel was over—*filled* (Genesis 29:21, JRL). A pregnancy could come to term—*be filled* (Genesis 25:24). Spaces, too, are filled to overflowing. When the Jordan River *fills* its banks during the time of harvest, it floods them beyond the brink (Joshua 3:15, JRL). When the hem of God's robe fills the temple, in Isaiah's grand vision, it's more than a ribbon of linen in the inner sanctum (Isaiah 6:1). *Filling* in Hebrew means what it says: making full, bringing to completion, fruition, wholeness, fullness.

Either experience—or both—may happen to you as you integrate these prayers to the Holy Spirit into your life. The Holy Spirit may break in from the outside, and you'll find your usual boundaries broken down. Or the Holy Spirit may gradually fill you to the brim with a vitality you never imagined, as your relationship with the Holy Spirit, little by little, becomes more personal, more intimate, more life-giving. Be alert to either experience of filling—or both—as you pray to the Holy Spirit day by day.

Brood

What is the very first action of the Spirit in the Bible? To brood. We might expect breathe or pour or clothe or rush upon or fill or inspire. But probably not brood. Nevertheless, Eugene Peterson perfectly translates the Hebrew verb, *rachaph*, in Genesis 1:2: "God's Spirit brooded like a bird above the watery abyss" (THE MESSAGE). Peterson translates the Hebrew verb in this way because the verb *brood* occurs elsewhere in the Old Testament, when God is portrayed "like an eagle hovering over its nest, overshadowing its young, Then spreading its wings, lifting them into the air, teaching them to fly" (Deuteronomy 32:11–12, THE MESSAGE).

When we first meet the Spirit, in the Bible's seventeenth word (in the original Hebrew), we glimpse a bird of prey plucking its young, carrying them to safety, and teaching them to fly. Chaos can't withstand the eagle's presence.

There is something magnificent, maybe even magical, in this first encounter with the Spirit. Here we are plunked into the abyss—a world teeming with distractions, swarming with obligations, overrun by chaos—and we desperately need moments of respite, quiet intervals of rest.

Welcome to a book that offers respite and rest. *But not escape.*

In lieu of escape, this book offers *encounter*. Engagement with the Holy Spirit, who broods over the bedlam of our lives, our world, like an eagle, with a vigilant eye—an *eagle* eye—and powerful pinions. So don't expect a retreat from this book, with its prayers to the Holy Spirit. You will find respite and rest, I'm sure. But expect engagement, too, every time you pray, "Holy Spirit."

Expect to learn how to fly.

PRAYERS FOR
MORNING

Holy Spirit

Let me not lose myself in tedium
errands
obligations.

Holy Spirit
Still me once in a while
Stop me sometimes
Let me breathe now and then.

Holy Spirit
Teach me to pray
Not many words
Just one: Abba.

Amen.

Galatians 4:4–7

But when the fullness of time had come, God sent his Son, born of a woman, born under the law, in order to redeem those who were under the law, so that we might receive adoption as children. And because you are children, God has sent the Spirit of his Son into our hearts, crying, "Abba! Father!" So you are no longer a slave but a child, and if a child then also an heir, through God. (NRSV)

Holy Spirit

Make me timely
  essential
  relevant.

Not relevant for its own sake—but substantial

Not optional—but essential

Not trendy—but timely.

Rooted in the time-tested traditions of faith
  Essential.
  Relevant.
  Inspired.

                              Amen.

1 Chronicles 12:18

Then the Spirit came upon Amasai, chief of the Thirty, and he said, "We are yours, O David; and with you, O son of Jesse! Peace, peace to you, and peace to the one who helps you! For your God is the one who helps you." Then David received them, and made them officers of his troops. (NRSV)

Holy Spirit

As long as I live, let me breathe out
    God's praise,
While I still live, let me exhale
    God's truth.

And with death around me,
        when health drops away,

Let me breathe out
    God's truth,
Let me sing, soft but strongly,
    God's praise.

    Amen.

Job 27:3–4

As long as my breath is in me
and the Spirit of God is in my nostrils,
my lips will not speak falsehood,
and my tongue will not utter deceit. (NRSV)

Holy Spirit

A daily practice of memory-making
Verses learned well,
inside and out.

A daily dose of meditation
Passages studied well,
backwards and forwards.

A daily diet of everyday education
Texts read well,
high and low.

Holy Spirit,

Ready me for inspiration,
mark me today as a companion of Jesus.

Amen.

Acts 4:8–12

Then Peter, filled with the Holy Spirit, said to them, "Rulers of the people and elders, if we are questioned today because of a good deed done to someone who was sick and are asked how this man has been healed, let it be known to all of you, and to all the people of Israel, that this man is standing before you in good health by the name of Jesus Christ of Nazareth, whom you crucified, whom God raised from the dead. This Jesus is 'the stone that was rejected by you, the builders; it has become the cornerstone.' There is salvation in no one else, for there is no other name under heaven given among mortals by which we must be saved." (NRSV)

Holy Spirit

You are capable of the spectacular, I know
inspiring mesmerizing sermons,
empowering breathtaking miracles.

But today, Holy Spirit, I pray for none of that.

Today, I pray that you, with the Father and the Son,
will embrace a shared purpose:
To fire in me a passion to obey
everything Jesus commanded.
To stir in me a passion to teach others to obey
everything Jesus commanded.

To forgive me when I don't obey.
To forgive them when they don't.

Today, Holy Spirit,
I pray for only that.

Amen.

Matthew 28:16–20

Now the eleven disciples went to Galilee, to the mountain to which Jesus had directed them. When they saw him, they worshiped him; but some doubted. And Jesus came and said to them, "All authority in heaven and on earth has been given to me. Go therefore and make disciples of all nations, baptizing them in the name of the Father and of the Son and of the Holy Spirit, and teaching them to obey everything that I have commanded you. And remember, I am with you always, to the end of the age." (NRSV)

Holy Spirit

Fiery ecstasy,
    Language maker:

Don't let me come unsuspecting to Pentecost
    or arrive ill-equipped at ecstasy.

Sharpen my will to study
Hone my mind to think
Whet my appetite to learn.

And when I part my lips
    and breathe out words
        God's praiseworthy acts—
        let them come first.

                Amen.

Acts 2:1–13

When the day of Pentecost had come, they were all together in one place. And suddenly from heaven there came a sound like the rush of a violent wind, and it filled the entire house where they were sitting. Divided tongues, as of fire, appeared among them, and a tongue rested on each of them. All of them were filled with the Holy Spirit and began to speak in other languages, as the Spirit gave them ability. Now there were devout Jews from every nation under heaven living in Jerusalem. And at this sound the crowd gathered and was bewildered, because each one heard them speaking in the native language of each. Amazed and astonished, they asked, "Are not all these who are speaking Galileans? And how is it that we hear, each of us, in our own native language? Parthians, Medes, Elamites, and residents of Mesopotamia, Judea and Cappadocia, Pontus and Asia, Phrygia and Pamphylia, Egypt and the parts of Libya belonging to Cyrene, and visitors from Rome, both Jews and proselytes, Cretans and Arabs—in our own languages we hear them speaking about God's deeds of power." All were amazed and perplexed, saying to one another, "What does this mean?" But others sneered and said, "They are filled with new wine." (NRSV)

Holy Spirit

I've no need for grand visions
    strategic plans
    blueprints for success.

Bury me instead among the faint
    the weary
    the worn.

I've no need for great speeches
    striking sermons
    thunderous applause.

Busy me instead with laughter
    a wordplay or two
    mirth.

                    Amen.

Isaiah 61:1–3

The Spirit of the Lord God is upon me, because the Lord has anointed me; he has sent me to bring good news to the oppressed, to bind up the brokenhearted, to proclaim liberty to the captives, and release to the prisoners; to proclaim the year of the Lord's favor, and the day of vengeance of our God; to comfort all who mourn; to provide for those who mourn in Zion—to give them a garland instead of ashes, the oil of gladness instead of mourning, the mantle of praise instead of a faint spirit. They will be called oaks of righteousness, the planting of the Lord, to display his glory. (nrsv)

Holy Spirit

I'm comfortable with clarity—if I'm honest,
    with clichés, too:
        politics and religion don't mix.

I'm happy to inhabit a world in which
    spiritual is mystical—even unworldly:
        politics and religion don't mix.

I'm satisfied with a private piety—a world apart:
        politics and religion don't mix.

Where then is the might?
Where then is the power?
Where then are you, Spirit?
Let me discover might in you, the Spirit.
Let me experience power in you, the Spirit.
Let me join the ranks of Wilberforce, Day, King
        a host of poets and saints
        and social reformers
        from ages past.

                Amen.

Zechariah 4:6

*[The angel] said to me, "This is the word of the L*ORD *to Zerubbabel: Not by might, nor by power, but by my spirit, says the L*ORD *of hosts." (*NRSV*)*

Holy Spirit

When we trip over success.

When we pursue power.

When we ache for achievements.

Wean us from success, babes that we are—
      or should be.

Wrest power from our grasp, children that we are—
      or should be.

Weaken our grip on achievements,
  sons and daughters that we are—
      or should be.

Train us to rejoice in the purest object of joy.

God. Alone.

                Amen.

Luke 10:21–24

At that same hour Jesus rejoiced in the Holy Spirit and said, "I thank you, Father, Lord of heaven and earth, because you have hidden these things from the wise and the intelligent and have revealed them to infants; yes, Father, for such was your gracious will. All things have been handed over to me by my Father; and no one knows who the Son is except the Father, or who the Father is except the Son and anyone to whom the Son chooses to reveal him." Then turning to the disciples, Jesus said to them privately, "Blessed are the eyes that see what you see! For I tell you that many prophets and kings desired to see what you see, but did not see it, and to hear what you hear, but did not hear it." (NRSV)

Holy Spirit

I depend upon you for inspiration,
the wind at my back
the breath in my lungs
the Spirit in my heart.

Guide me now not to depend upon you,
to pray without inspiration
to learn without exhilaration
to puzzle without enthusiasm.

So that I am ready for your future,
prepared to listen when you speak
primed to puzzle over experiences I can't understand
poised to leave when you tell me to go.

Amen.

Acts 10:9–10, 19–20

About noon the next day, as they were on their journey and approaching the city, Peter went up on the roof to pray. He became hungry and wanted something to eat; and while it was being prepared, he fell into a trance.

While Peter was still thinking about the vision, the Spirit said to him, "Look, three men are searching for you. Now get up, go down, and go with them without hesitation; for I have sent them." (NRSV)

Holy Spirit

Teach me to learn,

Inspire me to practice,

Stir me to drill in the ways of discipleship.

Holy Spirit,
As I learn, fill me with wisdom-of-heart.

As I practice, flood me with intelligence.

As I drill, drench me with knowledge.

So that I can be ready
At any moment

In any way

With any skill.

Amen.

Exodus 35:30–35

Then Moses said to the Israelites: See, the Lᴏʀᴅ has called by name Bezalel son of Uri son of Hur, of the tribe of Judah; he has filled him with divine Spirit, with skill, intelligence, and knowledge in every kind of craft, to devise artistic designs, to work in gold, silver, and bronze, in cutting stones for setting, and in carving wood, in every kind of craft. And he has inspired him to teach, both him and Oholiab son of Ahisamach, of the tribe of Dan. He has filled them with skill to do every kind of work done by an artisan or by a designer or by an embroiderer in blue, purple, and crimson yarns, and in fine linen, or by a weaver—by any sort of artisan or skilled designer. (ɴʀsᴠ)

Holy Spirit

My request is simple to pray but hard to practice.

Instill in me and my community a hunger for learning.

Root in me and my community an ear for prophecy.

Plant in me and my community the seed of generosity.

Build in me and my community
  a passion for diversity and difference.

Cultivate in me and my community the practices of
                   worship
                   fasting
                   prayer.

Pour in me and my community
  a healthy dollop of common sense.

                   Amen.

Acts 13:1–3

Now in the church at Antioch there were prophets and teachers: Barnabas, Simeon who was called Niger, Lucius of Cyrene, Manaen a member of the court of Herod the ruler, and Saul. While they were worshiping the Lord and fasting, the Holy Spirit said, "Set apart for me Barnabas and Saul for the work to which I have called them." Then after fasting and praying they laid their hands on them and sent them off. (NRSV)

PRAYERS FOR NIGHTTIME

Holy Spirit

I have nothing to ask of you,
Nothing to request from you,
Nothing to yearn for.

Nothing but this:

To let go of ambition,
To abandon acquisition,
Nothing to yearn for.

Nothing but you.

Amen.

Daniel 5:11–12

There is a man in your kingdom who is endowed with a spirit of the holy gods. In the days of your father he was found to have enlightenment, understanding, and wisdom like the wisdom of the gods. Your father, King Nebuchadnezzar, made him chief of the magicians, enchanters, Chaldeans, and diviners, because an excellent spirit, knowledge, and understanding to interpret dreams, explain riddles, and solve problems were found in this Daniel, whom the king named Belteshazzar. Now let Daniel be called, and he will give the interpretation. (NRSV)

Holy Spirit

Closer than my breathing
Nearer than my heartbeat

When I tuck myself away for fear of life
And hide from threats real and imagined

Consider my lost call, my vanishing purpose

And fill me deep
Like my dear friend's kiss.

Face to face with Jesus I'll receive you
Heart to heart with Jesus I'll breathe you in.

Amen.

John 20:19–23

When it was evening on that day, the first day of the week, and the doors of the house where the disciples had met were locked for fear of the Jews, Jesus came and stood among them and said, "Peace be with you." After he said this, he showed them his hands and his side. Then the disciples rejoiced when they saw the Lord. Jesus said to them again, "Peace be with you. As the Father has sent me, so I send you." When he had said this, he breathed into them and said to them, "Receive the Holy Spirit. If you forgive the sins of any, they are forgiven them; if you retain the sins of any, they are retained." (NRSV/JRL)

Holy Spirit

The audacity to argue—
  We ask for this.

The fearlessness to fight—
  We plead for this.

The daring to debate—
  We beg for this.

The courage to compromise—
  We pray for this.

    Above all, Holy Spirit,
    We pray for this.

            Amen.

Acts 15:28–29

For it has seemed good to the Holy Spirit and to us to impose on you no further burden than these essentials: that you abstain from what has been sacrificed to idols and from blood and from what is strangled and from fornication. If you keep yourselves from these, you will do well. Farewell. (NRSV)

Holy Spirit

Once
Just once

Knowing
Understanding
Clarity

Not a descent from on high
Not even a dove floating down from the clouds

Just knowing
Understanding
Clarity

An ascent from scripture
A conviction rising up from the soil of devotion

Knowing
Understanding
Clarity

Once
Just once, Holy Spirit.

Amen.

Luke 2:25

Now there was a man in Jerusalem whose name was Simeon; this man was righteous and devout, looking forward to the consolation of Israel, and the Holy Spirit rested on him. (NRSV)

Holy Spirit

Eagle stirring above creation

Dove descending into me

I am, like Jesus, God's delight

Like Jesus, prepared to lead
             on a throne
             to a cross.

Let me learn this

Slower perhaps than you would like

But learn this in the meantime

Dove descending into me

Eagle stirring above creation.

                    Amen.

Mark 1:9–11

In those days Jesus came from Nazareth of Galilee and was baptized by John in the Jordan. And just as he was coming up out of the water, he saw the heavens torn apart and the Spirit descending like a dove on him. And a voice came from heaven, "You are my Son, the Beloved; with you I am well pleased." (NRSV)

Holy Spirit

I am tempted to adore spirituality in the abstract
      to lift my eyes to heaven
      to worship an ethereal God.

Pull me back to earth, Holy Spirit,
      to a world of widows
      to charts and tables and food scraps.

Inspire me here, Holy Spirit, not there
Fill me on earth, Holy Spirit, not in heaven;

Breathe integrity into my chores
      vitality into my errands
      wisdom into my drudgery.

                 Amen.

Acts 6:1–6

Now during those days, when the disciples were increasing in number, the Hellenists complained against the Hebrews because their widows were being neglected in the daily distribution of food. And the twelve called together the whole community of the disciples and said, "It is not right that we should neglect the word of God in order to wait on tables. Therefore, friends, select from among yourselves seven men of good standing, full of the Spirit and of wisdom, whom we may appoint to this task, while we, for our part, will devote ourselves to prayer and to serving the word." What they said pleased the whole community, and they chose Stephen, a man full of faith and the Holy Spirit, together with Philip, Prochorus, Nicanor, Timon, Parmenas, and Nicolaus, a proselyte of Antioch. They had these men stand before the apostles, who prayed and laid their hands on them. (NRSV)

Holy Spirit

I'm not asking you to cause life or death to disappear
hardship or distress to vanish
persecution or peril to evaporate.

But you can settle fears within this soul of mine
this panicked heart
this anxious spirit.

Holy Spirit,
Banish the Unholy Spirit,
as real as you
but unwelcome.

You can quiet my qualms
Anxieties that dog my steps by day
Forebodings that haunt me by night.

Holy Spirit,
I'm not asking you to cause death or life to disappear
But to hearten me with the love of Christ
with a love for Christ.

Amen.

Romans 8:12–17

So don't you see that we don't owe this old do-it-yourself life one red cent. There's nothing in it for us, nothing at all. The best thing to do is give it a decent burial and get on with your new life. God's Spirit beckons. There are things to do and places to go! This resurrection life you received from God is not a timid, grave-tending life. It's adventurously expectant, greeting God with a childlike "What's next, Papa?" God's Spirit touches our spirits and confirms who we really are. We know who he is, and we know who we are: Father and children. And we know we are going to get what's coming to us—an unbelievable inheritance! We go through exactly what Christ goes through. If we go through the hard times with him, then we're certainly going to go through the good times with him! (THE MESSAGE)

PRAYERS FOR DISCERNMENT

Holy Spirit

Signs would be good
   wonders, too.
An occasional prophetic word won't hurt, either
   and I wouldn't object to taking down
      an evil empire.

But I'll ask just now for wisdom
   a Spirit of wisdom;
Strong hands on my shoulders won't hurt, either
   and I wouldn't object to leading
      a small band of good people.

Fill me with wisdom, Holy Spirit
   durable
      dependable
         Wisdom.
            Amen!

Deuteronomy 34:7–12

Moses was 120 years old when he died. His eyesight was sharp; he still walked with a spring in his step. The People of Israel wept for Moses in the Plains of Moab thirty days. Then the days of weeping and mourning for Moses came to an end. Joshua son of Nun was filled with the spirit of wisdom because Moses had laid his hands on him. The People of Israel listened obediently to him and did the same as when God had commanded Moses. No prophet has risen since in Israel like Moses, whom God knew face-to-face. Never since has there been anything like the signs and miracle-wonders that God sent him to do in Egypt, to Pharaoh, to all his servants, and to all his land—nothing to compare with that all-powerful hand of his and all the great and terrible things Moses did as every eye in Israel watched. (THE MESSAGE)

Holy Spirit

I've forgotten how to breathe deeply,

fearlessly,

joyfully,

Afraid as I am that life will come

and knock the wind right out of me.

Mid-breath.

So I breathe in small gasps,

quick huffs,

short sighs,

Afraid as I am that life will come

and knock the wind right out of me.

Mid-breath.

Gather a windstorm from the four corners of the earth.

Rattle my tired bones.

Stretch my weary sinews.

Renew my parched flesh.

And bring me back, Holy Spirit,

back to life,

back to living,

back to hope.   Amen.

Ezekiel 37:1–10

GOD grabbed me. GOD's Spirit took me up and sat me down in the middle of an open plain strewn with bones. He led me around and among them—a lot of bones! There were bones all over the plain—dry bones, bleached by the sun.

He said to me, "Son of man, can these bones live?"

I said, "Master GOD, only you know that."

"He said to me, "Prophesy over these bones: 'Dry bones, listen to the Message of GOD!'

GOD, the Master, told the dry bones, "Watch this: I'm bringing the breath of life to you and you'll come to life. I'll attach sinews to you, put meat on your bones, cover you with skin, and breathe life into you. You'll come alive and you'll realize that I am GOD!"

I prophesied just as I'd been commanded. As I prophesied, there was a sound and, oh, rustling! The bones moved and came together, bone to bone. I kept watching. Sinews formed, then muscles on the bones, then skin stretched over them. But they had no breath in them.

He said to me, "Prophesy to the breath. Prophesy, son of man. Tell the breath, 'GOD, the Master, says, Come from the four winds. Come, breath. Breathe on these slain bodies. Breathe life!'"

So I prophesied, just as he commanded me. The breath entered them and they came alive! They stood up on their feet, a huge army. (*THE MESSAGE*)

Holy Spirit

Renew my vision
          not to escape reality but to
infuse it with equity.

Refresh my hope
          not to avoid the world as it is but to
suffuse it with integrity.

Revive my faith
          not to sidestep misery but to
defuse it with impartiality.

                                        Amen.

Isaiah 11:1–5

*A shoot shall come out from the stump of Jesse, and a branch shall grow out of his roots. The Spirit of the L*ORD *shall rest on him, the spirit of wisdom and understanding, the spirit of counsel and might, the spirit of knowledge and the fear of the L*ORD*. His delight shall be in the fear of the L*ORD*. He shall not judge by what his eyes see, or decide by what his ears hear; but with righteousness he shall judge the poor, and decide with equity for the meek of the earth; he shall strike the earth with the rod of his mouth, and with the breath of his lips he shall kill the wicked. Righteousness shall be the belt around his waist, and faithfulness the belt around his loins. (*NRSV*)

Holy Spirit

However I pray, let me pray in earnest.

Wherever I pray, let me pray in truth.

Whenever I pray, let me pray in love.

However I speak, let me speak in earnest.

Wherever I speak, let me speak in truth.

Whenever I speak, let me speak in love.

Amen.

1 Corinthians 14:1–3

Pursue love and strive for the spiritual gifts, and especially that you may prophesy. For those who speak in a tongue do not speak to other people but to God; for nobody understands them, since they are speaking mysteries in the Spirit. On the other hand, those who prophesy speak to other people for their upbuilding and encouragement and consolation. (NRSV)

Holy Spirit

> I hanker after protection.
> I crave preservation.
> I treasure salvation.

> "Leave things as they are." That's my solemn prayer.

Holy Spirit,

> I'm not so fond of transformation.
> I'm not so hungry for adaptation.
> I'm not so keen on modification.

> "Leave things as they are." That's my earnest prayer.

But how can I ask you for this?
And how could you possibly answer this prayer?

What could I be thinking?
How little could I know you?

You're torrential.
We're sopping, sodden, soaked.
Caught in the downpour
> of your craving to transform us from inside out
>> and also from outside in.

>>>> Amen.

Isaiah 44:1–5

But now hear, O Jacob my servant, Israel whom I have chosen! Thus says the L<small>ORD</small> who made you, who formed you in the womb and will help you: Do not fear, O Jacob my servant, Jeshurun whom I have chosen. For I will pour water on the thirsty land, and streams on the dry ground; I will pour my spirit upon your descendants, and my blessing on your offspring. They shall spring up like a green tamarisk, like willows by flowing streams. This one will say, "I am the L<small>ORD</small>'s," another will be called by the name of Jacob, yet another will write on the hand, "The L<small>ORD</small>'s," and adopt the name of Israel. (<small>NRSV</small>)

Holy Spirit

teacher
care-giver
father and mother
brother and sister—

You are my silent partner in promise
my quiet companion in hope.

In anguish accompany me
in weakness walk with me

Until justice floods the earth
and knowledge drenches the coastlands

Until sick sparrows finally fly
and dimly burning wicks blaze fiercely.

Amen.

Isaiah 42:1–4

Here is my servant, whom I uphold, my chosen, in whom my soul delights; I have put my spirit upon him; he will bring forth justice to the nations. He will not cry or lift up his voice, or make it heard in the street; a bruised reed he will not break, and a dimly burning wick he will not quench; he will faithfully bring forth justice. He will not grow faint or be crushed until he has established justice in the earth; and the coastlands wait for his teaching. (NRSV)

Holy Spirit

Spirit of Jesus
Spirit of Truth:

Ignite in me a passion for the truth
Instill in me a craving for knowledge
Inspire in me a hunger for wisdom.

Not just any truth, random knowledge, indiscriminate wisdom
But the truth about Jesus
who barked at his mother
who cried like a baby
who wore the towel of a servant and washed feet
who prayed the night away
who broiled fish on a spring morning.

Come to me as
the Spirit of Truth
the Spirit of Jesus
Holy Spirit.

Amen.

John 4:23–24

But the hour is coming, and is now here, when the true worshipers will worship the Father in spirit and truth, for the Father seeks such as these to worship him. God is spirit, and those who worship him must worship in spirit and truth." (NRSV)

Holy Spirit

With your wind,
      stir my soul.

With your words,
      order my day,

With your wings,
      gather me in,

And I will be grateful;

            I will be glad.

                  Amen.

Genesis 1:1–2

In the beginning when God created the heavens and the earth, the earth was a formless void and darkness covered the face of the deep, while a wind from God swept over the face of the waters. (NRSV)

Holy Spirit

I dangle my toes in a pool of piety.
Not much risk there.
It's still light, joyful, tranquil.

Take me deeper into the dark
      desert nights,
      desolate days,
      despair.

Take me to the far side
      of grief,
      of silence,
      of disquiet.

Where I'll collapse into the goodness of God.

                Amen.

Luke 11:9–13

"So I say to you, Ask, and it will be given you; search, and you will find; knock, and the door will be opened for you. For everyone who asks receives, and everyone who searches finds, and for everyone who knocks, the door will be opened. Is there anyone among you who, if your child asks for a fish, will give a snake instead of a fish? Or if the child asks for an egg, will give a scorpion? If you then, who are evil, know how to give good gifts to your children, how much more will the heavenly Father give the Holy Spirit to those who ask him!" (NRSV)

Holy Spirit

While I may want a word of comfort
     a pat on the back
     an arm around my shoulder;

     Someone comforting
     Something comfortable
     A comforter, pure and simple;

Wean me from encouragement rooted in my situation
     from comfort controlled by my condition
     from reassurance restricted to my desolation.

Speak a word of encouragement
  rooted in Jesus' crucifixion
     comfort controlled by his exertion
     reassurance grounded in his resurrection.

Amen.

Acts 9:31

Meanwhile the church throughout Judea, Galilee, and Samaria had peace and was built up. Living in the fear of the Lord and in the comfort of the Holy Spirit, it increased in numbers. (NRSV)

Holy Spirit

I know they're not baubles, bangles, and beads
       not just sparklers on a summer night
       not bright and beautiful window displays
          that draw my eyes.

Miracles are more than that: the power of God
     healing, binding, freeing.

Still, given the choice,
       I'd choose the miracles
          healings
          flashes of ecstasy
          prophetic words.
       I'd opt for works of power right in front of my eyes.
       I'd gawk at signs and wonders.

But one miracle matters
     one wonder counts
     one sign signifies life.

Draw me to power made perfect in weakness
     to the energy of grace
     to the miracle of self-giving.

To Jesus, the crucified one.

                  Amen.

1 Corinthians 2:9–13

But, as it is written, "What no eye has seen, nor ear heard, nor the human heart conceived, what God has prepared for those who love him"—these things God has revealed to us through the Spirit; for the Spirit searches everything, even the depths of God. For what human being knows what is truly human except the human spirit that is within? So also no one comprehends what is truly God's except the Spirit of God. Now we have received not the spirit of the world, but the Spirit that is from God, so that we may understand the gifts bestowed on us by God. And we speak of these things in words not taught by human wisdom but taught by the Spirit, interpreting spiritual things to those who are spiritual. (NRSV)

PRAYERS FOR MOMENTS OF CRISIS

Holy Spirit, I panic.

    I forget to breathe,

        the impulses are so strong

           the forces relentless,

                the lure tenacious.

                    Irresistible, even.

                        When I forget to breathe,

                        breathe into me, Holy Spirit.

                Restore my equilibrium.

            rescue the rhythm of my soul,

        the beat of my heart.

    The body calmed, tranquil, at peace.

    Reminded to breathe.

I rest, Holy Spirit.

                        Amen.

1 Thessalonians 4:3–8

For this is the will of God, your sanctification: that you abstain from fornication; that each one of you know how to control your own body in holiness and honor, not with lustful passion, like the Gentiles who do not know God; that no one wrong or exploit a brother or sister in this matter, because the Lord is an avenger in all these things, just as we have already told you beforehand and solemnly warned you. For God did not call us to impurity but in holiness. Therefore whoever rejects this rejects not human authority but God, who also gives his Holy Spirit to you. (NRSV)

Holy Spirit

Gentle dove
Whispered love,

Don't let me linger where it's safe;

Throw me to raging lions
Drive me into festering hatreds
Banish me to terrible isolation;

But—

Come with me where isolation terrifies
Escort me where hatreds fester
Join me where lions rage;

Don't let me linger here protected

Fiery love
Forceful dove.

Amen.

Mark 1:12–13

And the Spirit immediately drove him out into the wilderness. He was in the wilderness forty days, tempted by Satan; and he was with the wild beasts; and the angels waited on him. (NRSV)

Holy Spirit, prompt me to wait,

        to pause

        to hear my own breath.

Holy Spirit, teach me to listen,

        to deliberate

        to consider your own breath.

Holy Spirit, prod me to speak

        in hushed tones

        in wisdom whispered.

                Amen.

Job 32:16–20

And am I to wait, because they do not speak, because they stand there, and answer no more? I also will give my answer; I also will declare my opinion. For I am full of words; the spirit within me constrains me. My heart is indeed like wine that has no vent; like new wineskins, it is ready to burst. I must speak, so that I may find relief; I must open my lips and answer. (NRSV)

Holy Spirit

Come to me!
Fill me!
Inspire me!

No, that's not right.
Be the source of wisdom in my life.
Become the spring of discernment throughout my days.
Mature in me as the Spirit of God.

Not just while my hands are held high in worship
But while they are cuffed by hardship.
In drudgery and setbacks,
In delays and interruptions,
Interminable waiting.

Yes, that's right, Holy Spirit. While life batters and bruises
Be the source of wisdom.
Become the spring of discernment.
Mature in me as the Spirit of God.

Amen.

Genesis 41:37–40

The proposal pleased Pharaoh and all his servants. Pharaoh said to his servants, "Can we find anyone else like this—one in whom is the Spirit of God?" So Pharaoh said to Joseph, "Since God has shown you all this, there is no one so discerning and wise as you. You shall be over my house, and all my people shall order themselves as you command; only with regard to the throne will I be greater than you." (NRSV)

Holy Spirit

You are not just a whirlwind in the desert,
　　a tempest in a teapot.

You are also here in the slow growth of learning,
　　a nearly imperceptible accrual of wisdom.

Holy Spirit,
　　Inspire me from the inside out,
　　　　With patience
　　　　　　Resolution
　　　　　　　　Stamina.

And I will be ready to work
　　To imagine
　　　　To spin,
　　　　　　To weave,
　　　　　　　　To dye,
　　　　　　　　　　To discover you
　　　　　　　　　　　　even in the desert.

　　　　　　　　　　Amen.

Exodus 28:1–3

Then bring near to you your brother Aaron, and his sons with him, from among the Israelites, to serve me as priests—Aaron and Aaron's sons, Nadab and Abihu, Eleazar and Ithamar. You shall make sacred vestments for the glorious adornment of your brother Aaron. And you shall speak to all who have ability, whom I have endowed with skill, that they make Aaron's vestments to consecrate him for my priesthood. (NRSV)

Holy Spirit

Train me to lead, but not alone
      to walk alongside, not in front.

Train me to follow, but not straggling
      to walk alongside, not behind.

Train me to accompany, shoulder to shoulder
      to walk alongside, all along the way nearby.

Amen.

Numbers 11:16–17, 24–25

So the LORD said to Moses, "Gather for me seventy of the elders of Israel, whom you know to be the elders of the people and officers over them; bring them to the tent of meeting, and have them take their place there with you. I will come down and talk with you there; and I will take some of the spirit that is on you and put it on them; and they shall bear the burden of the people along with you so that you will not bear it all by yourself. … So Moses went out and told the people the words of the LORD; and he gathered seventy elders of the people, and placed them all around the tent. Then the LORD came down in the cloud and spoke to him, and took some of the spirit that was on him and put it on the seventy elders; and when the spirit rested upon them, they prophesied. But they did not do so again. (NRSV)

Holy Spirit

When I am seized by self-interest
        snatched by smooth words,
        seduced by spiritual shortcuts;

Claim me, criticize me, call me back
        to justice—not dishonesty
        to power—not reliance on power
        to might—not the pretense of peace.

Call me back to an enduring experience of you.

                Amen.

Micah 3:5–8

Here is GOD's Message to the prophets, the preachers who lie to my people: "For as long as they're well paid and well fed, the prophets preach, 'Isn't life wonderful! Peace to all!' But if you don't pay up and jump on their bandwagon, their 'God bless you' turns into 'God damn you.' Therefore, you're going blind. You'll see nothing. You'll live in deep shadows and know nothing. The sun has set on the prophets. They've had their day; from now on it's night. Visionaries will be confused, experts will be all mixed up. They'll hide behind their reputations and make lame excuses to cover up their God-ignorance. But me—I'm filled with GOD's power, filled with GOD's Spirit of justice and strength, ready to confront Jacob's crime and Israel's sin." (THE MESSAGE)

Holy Spirit

> Air of human concord
>
> Heir of divine accord:

I belong to a church that has splintered

> a temple that has split
>
> a body that is scarred,

And I am seduced into schism

> by good reason
>
> with just cause;

But there is no reason good enough

> to scar the body
>
> to split the temple
>
> to splinter the church.

Forgive me for misplaced devotion

> and divided loyalties.

I have only one place to go—not many.

I have only one God to worship—not several.

I have only one Lord to serve—not scores.

I have only one Spirit to breathe—only one.

> Amen.

1 Corinthians 3:16–17

Do you not know that you are God's temple and that God's Spirit dwells in you? If anyone destroys God's temple, God will destroy that person. For God's temple is holy, and you are that temple. (NRSV)

Holy Spirit

I prefer order to chaos
        stability to bedlam
        stillness to mayhem.

Who wouldn't?

You wouldn't.

Divine cloudburst
Holy downpour
Sacred torrent

Topple my world with your benevolence
Barrage my barricades with your generosity
Flood my heart with your compassion.

Who can accomplish this?

You, Holy Spirit.

You!

            Amen.

Joel 2:28–29

Then afterward I will pour out my spirit on all flesh; your sons and your daughters shall prophesy, your old men shall dream dreams, and your young men shall see visions. Even on the male and female slaves, in those days, I will pour out my Spirit. (NRSV)

Holy Spirit

In disarray and darkness and death
    In betrayals and beatings and bereavement,

A whiff of truth
    A word for Jesus,

This is all I ask of you
    My soul's sole request
        My heart's heartfelt prayer.

Because to follow Jesus to the cross
  is the best of life
And to hear a solitary word from you
  is the best in death.

Just a whiff of truth,
And a word for Jesus, please.

    Amen.

Mark 13:9–13

As for yourselves, beware; for they will hand you over to councils; and you will be beaten in synagogues; and you will stand before governors and kings because of me, as a testimony to them. And the good news must first be proclaimed to all nations. When they bring you to trial and hand you over, do not worry beforehand about what you are to say; but say whatever is given you at that time, for it is not you who speak, but the Holy Spirit. Brother will betray brother to death, and a father his child, and children will rise against parents and have them put to death; and you will be hated by all because of my name. But the one who endures to the end will be saved. (NRSV)

PRAYERS FOR ANYTIME

Holy Spirit

Spirit of Jesus,
Spirit of learning,
Spirit of generosity,

I hope to be full, joyful, fulfilled;

And I am—but not quite.

I still need ears to hear,
I still need a parched throat craving you,
I still need empty pockets and open hands;

Hands open to receive you as a gift,
Open hands to give you to those who'll receive;

Those who'll receive you—
the Spirit of generosity
the Spirit of learning
the Spirit of Jesus—
Holy Spirit.

Amen.

Revelation 22:17

The Spirit and the bride say, "Come." And let everyone who hears say, "Come." And let everyone who is thirsty come. Let anyone who wishes take the water of life as a gift. (NRSV)

Holy Spirit

I want to be clean
> not just tidied up,
> dusted a bit
> straightened out.

I want to be squeaky clean
> fresh from a shower
> smelling like soap,
> like new.

I want to be clean from the inside out,
> the rhythmic beat of a new heart,
> the bright red of fresh blood,
> the pure joy of new life.

Holy, too.
Holy, like you, God's presence.

> Amen.

Psalm 51:10–12

God, make a fresh start in me,
    shape a Genesis week from the chaos of my life.
Don't throw me out with the trash,
    or fail to breathe holiness in me.
Bring me back from gray exile,
    put a fresh wind in my sails! (THE MESSAGE)

Create in me a clean heart, O God,
and put a new and right spirit within me.
Do not cast me away from your presence,
and do not take your holy spirit from me.
Restore to me the joy of your salvation,
and sustain in me a generous spirit. (NRSV)

Holy Spirit

grace and prayer I can handle—
being the Christian that I want to be,
but not this sort of grace and prayer—
being the Christian that I am.

grace to see my sin
head on
no holds barred;

prayer that reveals my sin
head on
no holds barred.

That grace and prayer I'm not so sure I want
to know I've wounded God deeply
parried, like it was just a game
that didn't matter much,
then pierced God's heart.

Holy Spirit, this is uncanny grace and unwelcome prayer.
My grief will match God's, won't it?
The retching of parents who've lost their child

Holy Spirit, this is raw grace
pure prayer
So take me there, to the heart of God. Amen.

Zechariah 12:8–10

On the Big Day, I'll look after everyone who lives in Jerusalem so that the lowliest, weakest person will be as glorious as David and the family of David itself will be god-like, like the Angel of GOD leading the people. On the Big Day, I'll make a clean sweep of all the godless nations that fought against Jerusalem. Next I'll deal with the family of David and those who live in Jerusalem. I'll pour a spirit of grace and prayer over them. They'll then be able to recognize me as the One they so grievously wounded—that piercing spear-thrust! And they'll weep—oh, how they'll weep! Deep mourning as of a parent grieving the loss of the firstborn child. (THE MESSAGE)

Holy Spirit

We've got work to do
   sleeves to roll up
   loins to gird.
We've got a temple to construct—with lives to restore.
We've got a nation to build—with broken souls to revive.
We've got a future to imagine—with damaged dreams to
   heal.

Stand, Holy Spirit
   not just before us—but in us,
   not just behind us—but among us,
   not just alongside us—but within us.

Lead, Holy Spirit
   like the pillar of fire that drove us
      from the slave pits of Egypt,
   like the pillar of cloud that steered us away
      from the tyranny of Pharaoh,
   like the angel of God's presence that piloted us
      from the captivity of empires.

Because we've got work to do
      loins to gird
      sleeves to roll up
   And you are ready—living and breathing among us
      right now.

                                        Amen.

Haggai 2:4–9

Yet now take courage, O Zerubbabel, says the LORD; take courage, O Joshua, son of Jehozadak, the high priest; take courage, all you people of the land, says the LORD; work, for I am with you, says the LORD of hosts, according to the promise that I made you when you came out of Egypt. My spirit abides among you; do not fear. For thus says the LORD of hosts: Once again, in a little while, I will shake the heavens and the earth and the sea and the dry land; and I will shake all the nations, so that the treasure of all nations shall come, and I will fill this house with splendor, says the LORD of hosts. The silver is mine, and the gold is mine, says the LORD of hosts. The latter splendor of this house shall be greater than the former, says the LORD of hosts; and in this place I will give prosperity, says the LORD of hosts. (NRSV)

Holy Spirit

The flames of Pentecost we know
    miracles and marvels
    tongues as of fire
    men and women dumbfounded—
      understanding the good news of
      God among us.

But a spark?
A spark of the Spirit?
Yes, a spark for mid-course correction
    reminders
      warning
        goodness
          trust.

You keep us on the straight and narrow
Sometimes, Holy Spirit, it's that simple.

A spark
    A flame
      A footpath
        A faith in the right direction.
          Amen.

Wisdom of Solomon 12:1–2

In all created beings, O Lord, you find a spark of your own immortal spirit. To those who wander from the straight and narrow, you provide mid-course correction. To those who sin against you, you give a sharp warning plus a hopeful word; you want everyone to leave the wicked life behind and believe in you. (THE MESSAGE)

For your immortal spirit is in all things. Therefore you correct little by little those who trespass, and you remind and warn them of the things through which they sin, so that they may be freed from wickedness and put their trust in you, O Lord. (NRSV)

Holy Spirit

It's a playground, this world of yours
      a swimming pool, this sea,
        this grass and dirt we frolic in—a sandbox.

We run till we are out of breath. We dart and dash till weary,
        happy in the setting sun of a good day's games

Until we can't breathe—and gasp our last gulp of air.

Back to the mud we go—but not in grassy games
        not in dirt scrubbed with a bar of soap

We're not just dirty, muddy from rolling and rollicking all day;

We are dirt—just mud, if you pull away.
        So don't. Please don't.

Full of you, we spring to life
Breathing you, we bloom and blossom

And discover a world with pet dragons
        where sardines, sharks and salmon play. Amen.

Psalm 104:24–30

What a wildly wonderful world, God!
*   *You made it all, with Wisdom at your side,*
*   *made earth overflow with your wonderful creations.*
Oh, look—the deep, wide sea,
*   *brimming with fish past counting, sardines and sharks*
*   *and salmon.*
Ships plow those waters,
*   *and Leviathan, your pet dragon, romps in them.*
All the creatures look expectantly to you to give them
*   *their meals on time.*
You come, and they gather around;
*   *you open your hand and they eat from it.*
If you turned your back, they'd die in a minute—
Take back your Spirit and they die,
*   *revert to original mud;*
Send out your Spirit and they spring to life—
*   *the whole countryside in bloom and blossom.*
(THE MESSAGE)

Holy Spirit

Fragile is all I can think about sometimes,
How we live in a cardboard universe that reads, this end up.

We spend our days in search of safety,
    our nights in quest of rest

But our world turns upside down anyway
We drop like a lead balloon

    Breathless—not with wonder
    But with worry—broken.

Turn our world right side up, Holy Spirit.
    Deserts into green fields
    Green fields into forests
    Wrong into Right
    War into Peace
    Curse into Blessing

Fill this cardboard universe with
your presence.
        Amen.

Isaiah 32:12–18

Take your stand, indolent women! Listen to me!

Indulgent, indolent women, listen closely to what I have to say.

In just a little over a year from now,

   you'll be shaken out of your lazy lives.

The grape harvest will fail, and there'll be no fruit on the trees.

Oh tremble, you indolent women.

   Get serious, you pampered dolls!

Strip down and discard your silk fineries. Put on funeral clothes.

Shed honest tears for the lost harvest, the failed vintage.

Weep for my people's gardens and farms that grow nothing but thistles and thornbushes.

Cry tears, real tears, for the happy homes no longer happy,

   the merry city no longer merry.

The royal palace is deserted, the bustling city quiet as a morgue,

The emptied parks and playgrounds taken over by wild animals, delighted with their new home.

Yes, weep and grieve until the Spirit is poured down on us from above

And the badlands desert grows crops and the fertile fields become forests.

Justice will move into the badlands desert. Right will build a home in the fertile field.

And where there's Right, there'll be Peace and the progeny of Right: quiet lives and endless trust.

My people will live in a peaceful neighborhood—in safe houses, in quiet gardens. (THE MESSAGE)

Holy Spirit

In one fell swoop you dash my desire to see you as
    something spiritual,
                divorced from the muck of reality

How?
By nearly causing a divorce
        by getting a young woman pregnant

Should I have put that more gently?
        More decently?
                More delicately?

No, Holy Spirit, no
        because, nine months down the line,
           Mary will feel anything but delicate,
                propped atop a lurching ass.

No, Holy Spirit, no
        because in the belly of a young woman is precisely
           where you want to be.

In our bellies, too.
In our livers and kidneys and spleens and hearts.
In our brains and bones and tongues and toes.
In our flesh. Incarnate.
                        Amen.

Matthew 1:18–23

The birth of Jesus took place like this. His mother, Mary, was engaged to be married to Joseph. Before they came to the marriage bed, Joseph discovered she was pregnant. (It was by the Holy Spirit, but he didn't know that.) Joseph, chagrined but noble, determined to take care of things quietly so Mary would not be disgraced. While he was trying to figure a way out, he had a dream. God's angel spoke in the dream: "Joseph, son of David, don't hesitate to get married. Mary's pregnancy is Spirit-conceived. God's Holy Spirit has made her pregnant. She will bring a son to birth, and when she does, you, Joseph, will name him Jesus—'God saves'—because he will save his people from their sins." This would bring the prophet's embryonic sermon to full term: Watch for this—a virgin will get pregnant and bear a son; they will name him Immanuel (Hebrew for "God is with us"). (THE MESSAGE)

Holy Spirit

Truth be told, I live
under a continuous, low-lying black cloud;
call it condemnation
call it sin
call it death.
To me, it's just a continuous, low-lying black cloud.

Holy Spirit,
Lift
the weight of condemnation
the impulse of sin
the tragedy of death
from my stooped shoulders.
I refuse to live any longer
under a continuous, low-lying black cloud.

Holy Spirit,
Blow
like a strong wind that magnificently clears the air
freeing me
from a fated lifetime of brutal tyranny
at the hands of sin and death.
I refuse to live any longer
under a continuous, low-lying black cloud.

Holy Spirit
Bracing wind
Breath of eternity
I refuse to live any longer
under a continuous, low-lying black cloud.   Amen.

Romans 7:25–8:2

So then, with my mind I am a slave to the law of God, but with my flesh I am a slave to the law of sin. There is therefore now no condemnation for those who are in Christ Jesus. For the law of the Spirit of life in Christ Jesus has set you free from the law of sin and of death. (NRSV)

Holy Spirit

You breathed on creation and beings began to move
You breathed, gulls soared.
You breathed, salmon spawned.
You breathed, frogs leaped.
You breathed, lions roared.

You breathed, man quivered in the mud
toes wiggling
arms reaching
heart pulsing
nose breathing.

You breathed, woman rose in the air
knees wobbling
hands flexing
lungs heaving
eyes blinking.

Breathe, Holy Spirit, breathe now.

Breathe on me outside the Garden.

Breathe on me far from Paradise.

Breathe on me East of Eden.

Breathe on me now, Holy Spirit

and I will

wiggle

reach

pulse

breathe

wobble

flex

heave

blink.

Breathe now, Holy Spirit,

for when you breathe on creation,

beings begin to move.

Amen.

Judith 16:13–16

I'll Praise my God with a new hymn:
  "Lord, great and bright, invincible, unbeatable.
May every creature serve you! You spoke over the void;
  creation appeared.
You breathed on creation; beings began to move. Who will tell you 'no'?
Under your unhesitating gaze, mountains quivered, boulders sagged.
But those who feared you will feel your warmth.
Great sacrifices may emit heavenly aromas,
  but small sacrifice still has something to offer the Lord!
Just take the Lord at his word, and you'll feel his warmth forever."

(THE MESSAGE)

Index of First Lines

Index of Scripture

NEW TESTAMENT

ABOUT PARACLETE PRESS

WHO WE ARE

Paraclete Press is a publisher of books, recordings, and DVDs on Christian spirituality. Our publishing represents a full expression of Christian belief and practice—from Catholic to Evangelical, from Protestant to Orthodox.

We are the publishing arm of the Community of Jesus, an ecumenical monastic community in the Benedictine tradition. As such, we are uniquely positioned in the marketplace without connection to a large corporation and with informal relationships to many branches and denominations of faith.

WHAT WE ARE DOING

Paraclete Press Books

Paraclete publishes books that show the richness and depth of what it means to be Christian. Although Benedictine spirituality is at the heart of all that we do, we publish books that reflect the Christian experience across many cultures, time periods, and houses of worship. We publish books that nourish the vibrant life of the church and its people.

We have several different series, including the best-selling Paraclete Essentials and Paraclete Giants series of classic texts in contemporary English; Voices from the Monastery—men and women monastics writing about living a spiritual life today; award-winning poetry; best-selling gift books for children on the occasions of baptism and first communion; and the Active Prayer Series that brings creativity and liveliness to any life of prayer.

Mount Tabor Books

Paraclete's newest series, Mount Tabor Books, focuses on liturgical worship, art and art history, ecumenism, and the first millennium church; and was created in conjunction with the Mount Tabor Ecumenical Centre for Art and Spirituality in Barga, Italy.

Paraclete Recordings

From Gregorian chant to contemporary American choral works, our recordings celebrate the best of sacred choral music composed through the centuries that create a space for heaven and earth to intersect. Paraclete Recordings is the record label representing the internationally acclaimed choir Gloriæ Dei Cantores, praised for their "rapt and fathomless spiritual intensity" by *American Record Guide*; the Gloriæ Dei Cantores Schola, specializing in the study and performance of Gregorian chant; and the other instrumental artists of the Gloriæ Dei Artes Foundation.

Paraclete Press is also privileged to be the exclusive North American distributor of the recordings of the Monastic Choir of St. Peter's Abbey in Solesmes, France, long considered to be a leading authority on Gregorian chant.

Paraclete Video

Our DVDs offer spiritual help, healing, and biblical guidance for a broad range of life issues including grief and loss, marriage, forgiveness, facing death, bullying, addictions, Alzheimer's, and spiritual formation.

Learn more about us at our website
www.paracletepress.com or
phone us toll-free at 1.800.451.5006

 SCAN
TO
READ
MORE

You may also be interested in:

Fresh Air
The Holy Spirit for an Inspired Life

Jack Levison

ISBN: 978-1-61261-068-9, $15.99, Paperback

Written in brief chapters, this book finds the presence of the Holy Spirit where we least expect it—in human breathing, in social transformation, in community, in hostile situations, and in serious learning. *Fresh Air* will unsettle and invigorate readers poised for a fresh experience of an ancient, confusing topic.

40 Days with the Holy Spirit

Jack Levison

ISBN: 978-1-61261-638-4, $16.99, Paperback

40 Days with the Holy Spirit will inspire you to encounter God in fresh and surprising ways. The book offers the opportunity to write and pray each day, is rooted in a rigorous study of Scripture, and includes 20–30 minute daily exercises with original prayers, that capture each day's insight into the deep, spiritual work of the Holy Spirit.

The Chants of the Holy Spirit

Gloriæ Dei Cantores Schola

ISBN: 978-1-61261-299-7, $18.95, SACD

The disciples waiting in the Upper Room, the rush of wind, the tongues of fire, and the spreading of the Gospel are all depicted in these Gregorian chants from two masses for the Feast of Pentecost.

Available from most booksellers or through Paraclete Press:
www.paracletepress.com 1-800-451-5006
Try your local bookstore first.